The

Let's

Whic

is the Giant

Can we see him?

What do you think the Giant Jumperee is?

BASSETT HOUSE SCHOOL

The back cover

Let's read the blurb together. This gives us some idea of what the play is about.

Who do you think the characters in the play are?

The title page

Let's read the title again.

The name of the playwright is Julia Donaldson and the name of the illustrator is Trevor Dunton.

1

Read page 2

Purpose: To identify the characters in the play.

Pause at page 2

Who are all these creatures? (Try to elicit the term 'characters'.)

Let's read the names of the characters.

Read pages 3 and 4 (Scene One)

Purpose: To find out about types of text in a play.
To find out where the Giant Jumperee is hiding.

Pause at page 4

Which scene is this?

Ask the children to point out the different types of text (fonts) on page 3.

What does the italic text tell us? (*what is happening and where*)

What does the bold text tell us? (*character names*)

Explain that the rest of the text is what each character says.

Where is the Giant Jumperee hiding? (*burrow*)

Is Rabbit scared? How can you tell? What does Cat say he will do?

How should we say the Giant Jumperee's speech? How can you tell?

Read pages 5 and 6 (Scene Two)

Purpose: To find out if Cat pounces on the Giant Jumperee.

Pause at page 6

What does the Giant Jumperee shout?

Does Cat pounce on the Giant Jumperee? What happens instead?

Which animal comes along next?

Scene Two

Cat goes up to the burrow.
She hears a loud voice.

Jumperee: I'M THE GIANT JUMPEREE
AND I'LL SQUASH YOU LIKE A FLEA!

Cat: Help! Help!

Bear comes along.

Bear: What's the matter, Cat?

Cat: There's a Giant Jumperee
in Rabbit's burrow.

Bear: Don't worry, I can knock him down!

Read pages 7 and 8 (Scene Three)

Purpose: To find out if Bear knocks down the Giant Jumperee.

Pause at page 8

What does the Giant Jumperee say?

Does Bear knock down the Giant Jumperee?

Was bear scared? Which animal does Bear meet?

What does Elephant say he will do? Read Elephant's words with expression.

What do you think will happen when Elephant meets the Giant Jumperee?

Scene Three

Bear goes up to the burrow.
He hears a loud voice.

Jumperee: I'M THE GIANT JUMPEREE
AND I'LL STING YOU LIKE A BEE!

Bear: Help! Help!

Elephant comes along.

Elephant: What's the matter, Bear?

Bear: There's a Giant Jumperee in Rabbit's burrow.

Elephant: Don't worry, I can pick him up with my trunk and toss him away.

Read pages 9 to 11 (Scene Four)

Purpose: To find out if Elephant picks up the Giant Jumperee with his trunk and tosses him away.

Pause at page 11

What happens to Elephant?

What do the other animals tell Frog? What do you think will happen to Frog?

What are the rhyming words on page 11?
(*be, flea, bee, tree*)

Scene Four

*Elephant goes up to the burrow.
She hears a loud voice.*

Jumperee: I'M THE GIANT JUMPEREE
AND I'M TALLER THAN A TREE!

Elephant: Help! Help!

Frog comes along.

Frog: What's the matter, Elephant?

Elephant: There's a Giant Jumperee
in Rabbit's burrow.

Rabbit: You'd better run, Frog.
He's as scary as can be.

Cat: He can squash you like a flea.

Bear: He can sting you like a bee.

Elephant: And he's taller than a tree.

READ

Read pages 12 and 13 (Scene Five)

Purpose: To find out if Frog can reveal who the Giant Jumperee is.

PAUSE

Pause at page 13

How do you think Frog feels?

What does Frog say to the Jumperee?

What happens next?

Do you think Frog knows who is in the burrow? How can you tell?

Who do you think the Jumperee is?

Scene Five

Frog goes up to the burrow.
She hears a loud voice.

Jumperee: I'M THE GIANT JUMPEREE AND YOU'RE TERRIFIED OF ME!

Frog: I'm not so sure about that! Why don't you come out, so I can see if I'm terrified or not?

Elephant, Bear, Cat, Rabbit: No! Don't come out! Help!

Elephant, Bear, Cat and Rabbit run away.

Frog looks into the burrow.

Frog: Well, Jumperee, are you coming out?

Frog waits for an answer.

Read pages 14 and 15

Purpose: To try and guess who the Giant Jumperee is.

Pause at page 15

Were you right about the Giant Jumperee?

How could you tell?

How do the animals feel on page 14? How do they feel when they see who the Giant Jumperee is?

Frog: You're the one we want to see, so we're counting up to three.

Elephant, Bear, Cat, Rabbit, Frog: One . . . two . . . THREE!

Baby Frog: Hello Mum! I'm the Giant Jumperee!

Frog: And you're coming home for tea!

Read to the end

Purpose: To find out how everyone feels now the Jumperee is revealed.

Pause at page 16

Where's the Jumperee going?
Do you think the animals mind that the Jumperee scared them?

After Reading

Revisit and Respond

T Re-read as a play with children taking the parts of different characters.

T Ask the children in groups to go through the book, discussing and listing play features (e.g. *character list, scenes, dialogue layout, stage directions*).

T Ask the children to discuss how they feel when someone shouts at them, drawing on personal experience.

W Ask the children to read through the book, and find all the rhyming words (e.g. *Jumperee, bee, tree, three, see, be, flea, tea*).

W Point out to the children that the rhyming words all end with the same sound – a long 'e' which is spelt in a variety of ways, i.e. 'ea', 'ee' and 'e'. Discuss the variations in spelling.

Follow-up

Independent Group Activity Work

This book is accompanied by two photocopy masters, one with a reading focus, and one with a writing focus, which support the main teaching objectives of this book. The photocopy masters can be found in the Planning and Assessment Guide.

PCM 15 (*reading*)

PCM 16 (*writing*)

Writing

Guided writing: How do you feel when someone shouts at you? Drawing on your own experience, write a short play with one character shouting and the other answering.

Extended writing: Write the play as a story from the Baby Frog's point of view. Write about how Baby Frog was able to scare the large animals by shouting.

Assessment Points

Assess that the children have learnt the main teaching points of the book by checking that they can:

- understand and identify elements of play format: characters, scenes, text formats
- recognize and read rhyming words
- identify and read words with long 'e' phoneme and its spelling variations.